WRINGER

by
Jerry Spinelli

Teacher Guide

Written by
Elizabeth M. Klar
and Cheryl Klar-Trim

Note

The FIrst Harper Trophy edition, 1998, published by HarperCollins Publishers Inc., ©1997 by Jerry Spinelli, was used to prepare this guide. The page references may differ in the hardcover or other paperback editions.

Please note: Please assess the appropriateness of this book for the age level and maturity of your students prior to reading and discussing it with your class.

ISBN 1-58130-676-8

Printed in the United States of America.

To order, contact your local school supply store, or—

Novel Units, Inc.
P.O. Box 433
Bulverde, TX 78163-0433

Web site: www.educyberstor.com

Table of Contents

Skills and Strategies

Thinking
Identifying attributes, research, compare/contrast, creative thinking, and critical thinking

Comprehension
Predicting, sequencing, foreshadowing, and anticipating

Vocabulary
Target words, word maps, synonyms, antonyms, and context clues

Listening/Speaking
Dramatizing, interviewing, storytelling, discussion, and music

Literary Elements
Literary analysis, setting, story mapping, plot development, and characterization

Writing
Character journal, personal writing, newspapers, creative writing, and acrostic poetry

Across the Curriculum
Social Studies–maps, research; Science, Math, Art–drawing, puppet making, design and color, diorama, collage, poetry, and comic strips

Summary

Wringer tells the story of Palmer LaRue, a nine-year-old boy who is apprehensive about his tenth birthday. When a boy turns ten, he is ready to become a wringer, which is a sign of honor. Wringers are used in Palmer's hometown, Waymer, where they celebrate an annual Family Fest in which five thousand pigeons are used for target practice. Palmer does not want to be a wringer, but he does want to belong. Palmer must make some hard decisions and stop being afraid when he becomes attached to a pet pigeon.

About the Author

Jerry Spinelli, a graduate of Gettysburg College, is an award-winning author of contemporary children's literature. Spinelli books include: *Maniac Magee, Space Station Seventh Grade, Jason and Marceline, Who Put That Hair in My Toothbrush?, There's a Girl in My Hammerlock, Crash,* and *The Library Card.* A father of six children, he often uses his own life experiences to write his novels. Jerry Spinelli's wife is also an author.

Introductory Activities

1. **Previewing the book:** Have students look at the cover and answer the journalist's questions about what they see: Who? Where? What? and Why? Based on their answers, students predict what the book will be about.

2. **Predicting the story:** Given the following clues, students write a paragraph predicting what they think will happen in the story.

   tradition   father   courage   loyalty   friendship

3. **Character Journal:** List the main characters from *Wringer* and have students choose one. As they read the book, students should write regular journal entries from that character's point of view reflecting on the events of the story. At various points in their reading, have students share their journals with classmates.

4. **Attribute Web:** Create an Attribute Web (p. 8 of this guide) with students for each of the following ideas: friends, decision, bravery, love, and birthday. Ask students to quickly tell what each word brings to mind. Encourage students to elaborate on particular ideas.

5. **Prediction Chart:** Have students set up a Prediction Chart (pp. 6-7 of this guide) to use as they read the book.

6. **Anticipation Questions:** Have students respond to each of the following statements with a "thumbs-up" (I agree) or a "thumbs-down" (I disagree) and discuss their responses.
   - Children should always do what their friends do.
   - You should never tell lies.
   - Secrets are made to tell.
   - It is wrong to kill for sport.
   - Friends should help and support each other.
   - You should think for yourself.
   - Love is shown in different ways.

Vocabulary Activities

1. **Target Word Charades:** Have students act out some of the vocabulary words and have classmates guess the target word. Some suggested words for *Wringer*:

woozy (18)	befuddled (36)	wobbled (56)	ambled (83)
recoiled (100)	snickered (130)	leering (152)	cringed (173)
lurking (198)	rotated (213)		

2. **Target Word Maps:** Have students complete word maps for vocabulary words of a certain part of speech. For example adjectives from *Wringer* would include:

crusty (8)	fiery (59)	classic (67)	syrupy (69)
raucous (119)	dopey (162)	precious (182)	reconstituted (205)

Word Map for an adjective

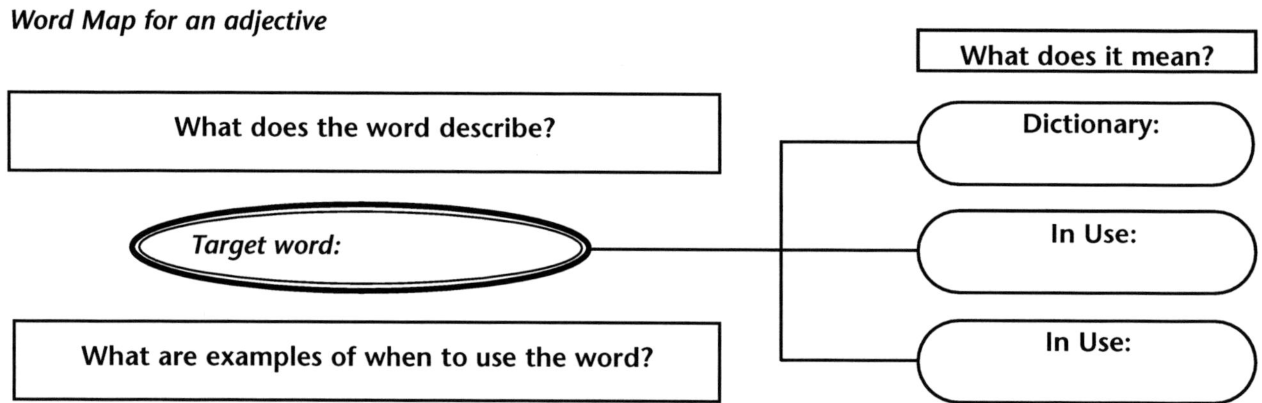

3. **Sentences:** Have students select five or six vocabulary words and use as many of the words as possible in one sentence.

4. **Synonym Match:** Have students select vocabulary words from a chapter and list one synonym for each vocabulary word on a small piece of paper. Mix the papers and have the students match each synonym to the appropriate vocabulary word.

5. **Odd One Out:** Use vocabulary words from one or two chapters. Have the students make a chain of four words. One word in the chain is the vocabulary word, two words are synonyms for the vocabulary word, and one word does not go with the others. (Mix the sequence of the words in the chain.) Students should exchange their chains and underline the word that does not belong with the others and explain why it does not belong.

6. **Vocabulary Sort:** Have the students sort vocabulary words into categories (e.g., nouns, verbs, and adjectives/adverbs).

7. **Vocabulary Boxes:** Cut a pattern for a cube (pattern included) from construction paper. Before the cube is glued together, each face should contain one of the following: a vocabulary word, the definition of the word, illustration of the word, a synonym of the word, antonym of the word, a sentence using the word. Display the vocabulary boxes in the room.

8. **Star Match:** Have students cut large golden stars from construction paper. The students should write a vocabulary word on one side of the star and its definition on the other side. Glue a piece of Velcro on the word side of the star. Attach the star to a bulletin board that has been covered with felt. Teams or individual students will choose a star (definitions are written on the front side). If the student can say the vocabulary word that matches the definition, he/she may keep the star. The team or individual with the most stars wins the game.

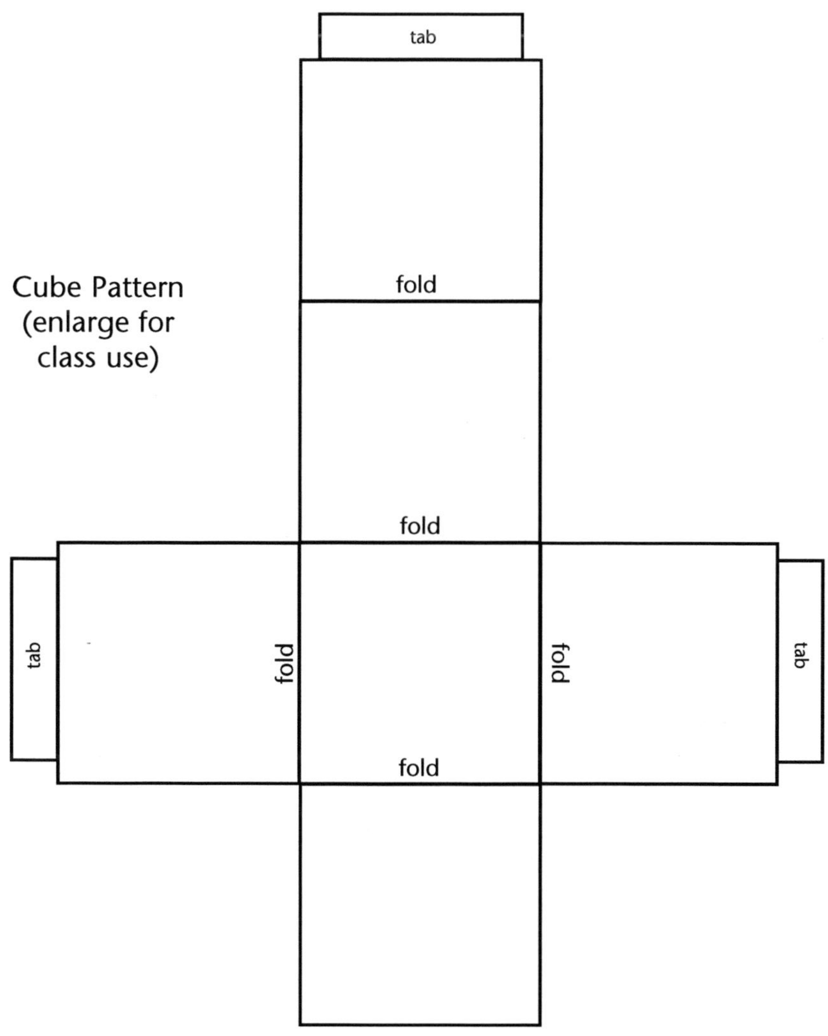

Cube Pattern (enlarge for class use)

Using Predictions in the Novel Unit Approach

We all make predictions as we read—little guesses about what will happen next, how a conflict will be resolved, which details will be important to the plot, which details will help fill in our sense of a character. Students should be encouraged to predict, to make sensible guesses as they read the novel.

As students work on their predictions, these discussion questions can be used to guide them: What are some of the ways to predict? What is the process of a sophisticated reader's thinking and predicting? What clues does an author give to help us make predictions? Why are some predictions more likely to be accurate than others?

Create a chart for recording predictions. This could be either an individual or class activity. As each subsequent chapter is discussed, students can review and correct their previous predictions about plot and characters as necessary.

Use the facts and ideas the author gives.

Use your own prior knowledge.

Apply any new information (i.e., from class discussion) that may cause you to change your mind.

Predictions:

____

____

____

____

Prediction Chart

What characters have we met so far?	What is the conflict in the story?	What are your predictions?	Why did you make those predictions?

Attribute Web

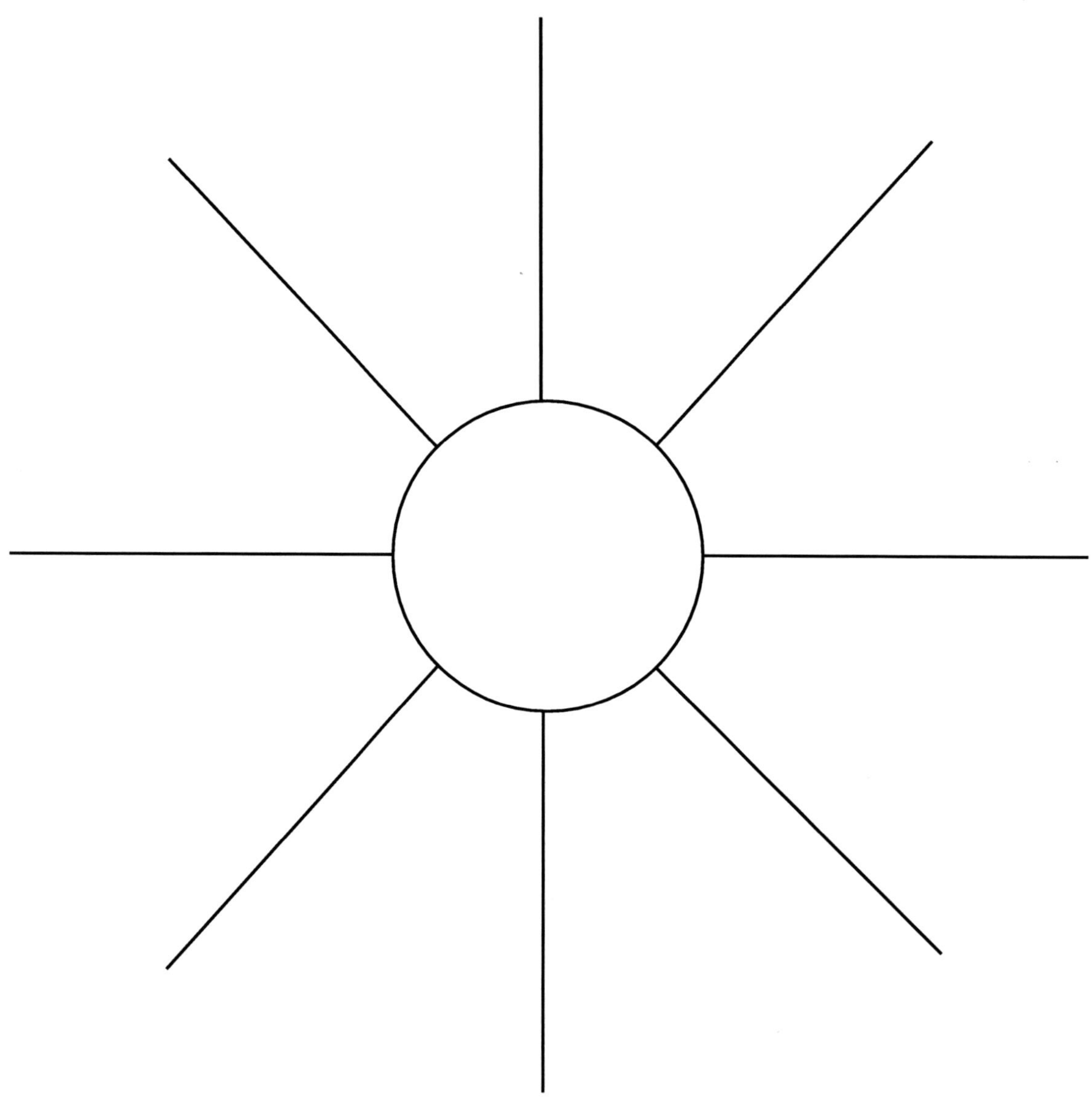

Using Character Webs in the Novel Unit Approach

Attribute webs are simply a visual representation of a character from the novel. They provide a systematic way for students to organize and recap the information they have about a particular character. Attribute webs may be used after reading the novel to recapitulate information about a particular character, or completed gradually as information unfolds. They may be completed individually or as a group project.

One type of character attribute web uses these divisions:

- How a character acts and feels. (How does the character act? How do you think the character feels? How would you feel if this happened to you?)
- How a character looks. (Close your eyes and picture the character. Describe him/her to me.)
- Where a character lives. (Where and when does the character live?)
- How others feel about the character. (How does another specific character feel about our character?)

In group discussion about the characters described in student attribute webs, the teacher can ask for backup proof from the novel. Inferential thinking can be included in the discussion.

Attribute webs need not be confined to characters. They may also be used to organize information about a concept, object, or place.

Character Attribute Web

The attribute web below will help you gather clues the author provides about a character in the novel. Fill in the blanks with words and phrases which tell how the character acts and looks, as well as what the character says and what others say about him or her.

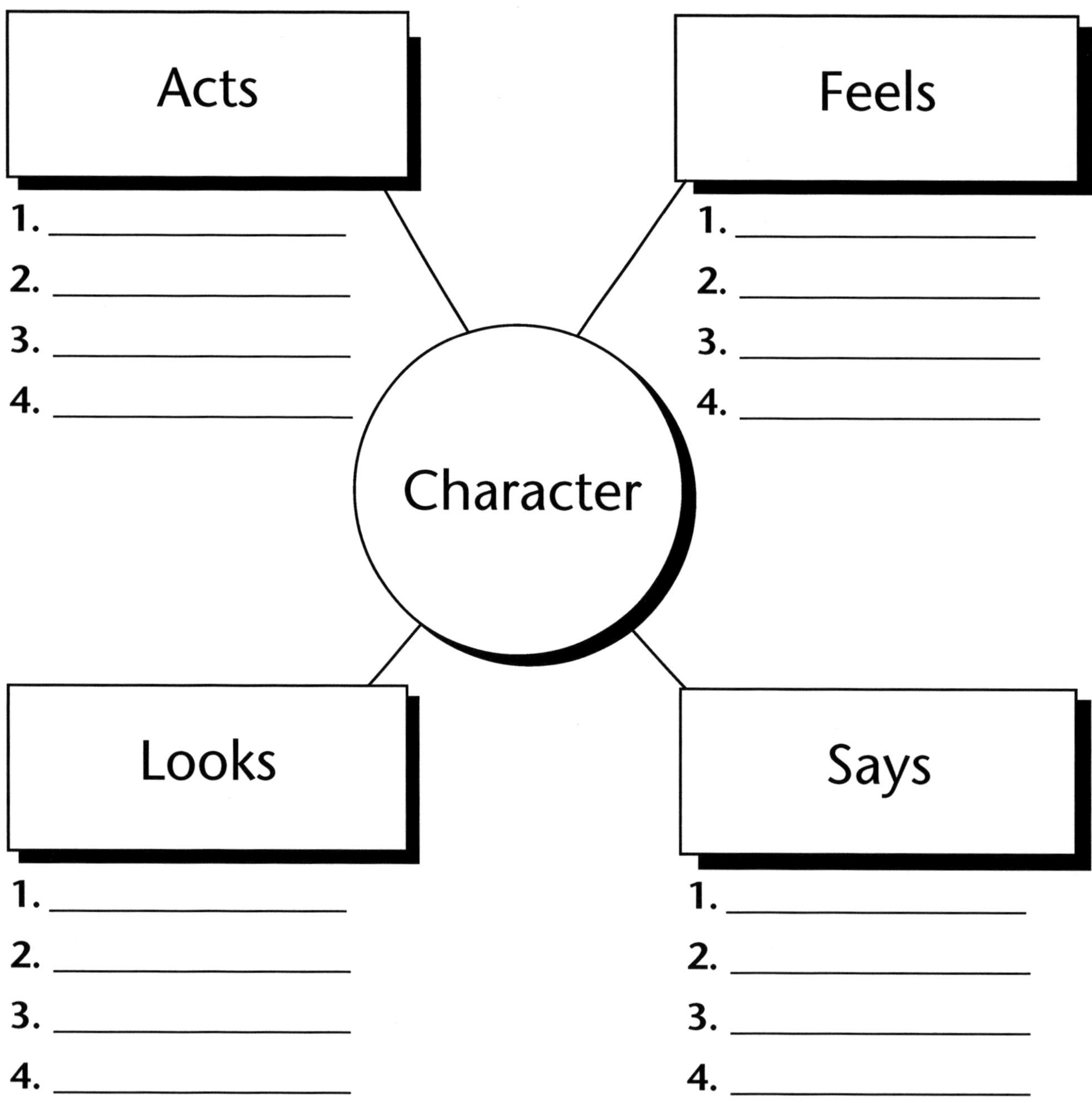

Story Map

Setting

Characters______________________________

____

Time and Place______________________________

____

Problem

Problem______________________________

____

____

Goal

Goal______________________________

____

____

Episodes

Beginning ⟶ Development ⟶ Outcome

____

____

____

____

Resolution

Resolution______________________________

____

____

____

Section One, Chapters 1-4

Vocabulary

rural (1)	frolicking (1)	climax (1)	punctured (3)
grub (6)	cackled (7)	piped (8)	crusty (8)
wick (10)	hoodlums (11)	booted (12)	rumbled (12)
smirk (12)	cringed (13)	veered (16)	lurched (16)
tilted (16)	meekest (17)	careening (17)	woozy (18)
hovered (18)			

Discussion Questions

1. How does Palmer feel about being a wringer? *(He does not want to be a wringer. The thought of becoming a wringer torments him.)*
2. Why does Palmer sometimes wish "this thing he did not want to be" would come after him? *(He could run from it and hide rather than wait until he has to face it.)*
3. How does Palmer feel when Beans, Mutto, and Henry show up at his house for his birthday? *(He cries tears of relief and joy because he was afraid they would not come.)*
4. Why doesn't Palmer's mother like Beans? *(She thinks he is a sneak and a troublemaker with a mean streak.)*
5. How does Palmer feel about the presents Beans, Mutto, and Henry give him? *(Palmer likes them as much as the presents his mother gives him because he knows they wouldn't have brought presents at all if they didn't want him to hang out with them.)*
6. What significance does receiving a nickname from Beans, Mutto, and Henry have for Palmer? *(It means Palmer has been accepted.)*
7. Why doesn't Palmer's mother want Beans, Mutto, and Henry to be in her house for very long? *(She thinks they are troublemakers.)*
8. Why do you think the boys harass Dorothy Gruzik? *(Answers will vary.)*
9. Why isn't Palmer interested in being friends with Dorothy? *(She is a girl and is a whole year younger.)*
10. How does Palmer feel when he runs with the gang for the first time? *(He shivers with excitement.)*
11. Why doesn't Palmer like the soccer field at the park? *(That is where the shooting on Pigeon Day takes place and Palmer is horrified by the thought of it.)*
12. How does Palmer feel when Beans and Mutto pretend to break Henry's neck while Henry acts like a wounded pigeon? *(Answers will vary.)*
13. How does Palmer react as the memories of Pigeon Day from three years earlier come back? *(At first he stands alone, frozen on the field. Then he runs off.)*

Supplementary Activities

1. Literary Analysis/Story Map: Have students begin a story map (p. 11 of this guide) to use as they read this story. As they continue reading, they should add new information about the characters, setting, problems, and events of the story.
2. Literary Analysis/Character: Have students begin an attribute web (p. 10 of this guide) for each major character in the story. Students should continue adding information to the webs as they read the story.
3. Art/Creative Thinking: Palmer celebrates his birthday by inviting his friends over for cake and ice cream. Discuss what information should be on an invitation. Have each student design an invitation to Palmer's party.

Section Two, Chapters 5-8

Vocabulary

legendary (20)	ultimate (21)	zombies (21)	hotfoot (23)
bashed (25)	gravely (26)	daintily (27)	bluntly (28)
warpath (28)	tingled (31)	boulevard (33)	squeamish (33)
diminishing (34)	taunt (36)	befuddled (36)	bewildered (39)
spewing (39)	hobbling (39)	etched (42)	teeming (42)

Discussion Questions

1. What does Palmer's mother say is the proper way to slide? How does it differ from the way Beans wants to slide? *(Mrs. LaRue wants Palmer to hold tight to the rail, no sliding down stacked or headfirst. Beans wants to slide down headfirst with all four boys stacked.)*
2. How does Palmer feel about his friends as they slide, stacked together? *(He feels his friends are depending on him.)*
3. Who seems to be the leader of the group? How can you tell? *(The other boys follow Beans and do what he does.)*
4. How do the boys react when Beans yells, "Ehh, yer old man!" to a lady on the playground? *(They start yelling it, too.)*
5. How does Palmer feel about The Treatment? *(He thinks receiving it is an honor and will win him the respect of others.)*
6. Why doesn't Palmer watch as he receives The Treatment? *(He has always heard it was best not to look if you got The Treatment.)*
7. How does Palmer's father react to Palmer receiving The Treatment? How does his mother react? *(His father acts as if he is proud; it is tradition in the neighborhood and he received it when he was young. His mother is upset and thinks it is awful that Palmer has been hurt.)*

8. Why doesn't Farquar give Palmer "an extra" like Beans and Mutto want? *(Farquar says that Palmer isn't really crying, he just has eye tears, and everybody gets them.)*

9. Do you think Farquar respects Palmer? *(Answers will vary.)*

10. How does Palmer react when his mother tells him that Dorothy is one of his best friends? *(He tells her she isn't and he would probably never see her if she didn't live across the street.)*

11. Why does Palmer think that "Henry" must be a nickname even though it sounds like a real name? *(He can't imagine that Beans would let Henry keep his real name and not give him a nickname.)*

12. What is special about the gift Palmer's father gives him? *(The toy soldiers have been passed down from father to son starting with Palmer's great-grandfather.)*

13. Why does Palmer think he has had a lot to overcome? *(He is the youngest, the shortest, and has an odd first name.)*

14. Why does Palmer begin crying inconsolably while brushing his teeth? *(He realizes that he has run out of birthdays and will be a wringer next year.)*

15. Why does Palmer feel like the grand marshal in a parade? *(Everyone is paying attention to him and is impressed because he received The Treatment.)*

16. Why is Palmer disappointed when the bruises on his arm start to heal? *(He likes being the center of attention and being respected for getting The Treatment.)*

17. Why is Dorothy mad at Palmer? *(He did not invite her to his birthday party.)*

18. Why doesn't Palmer feel as bad as he used to when his friends tease Dorothy? *(He is mad at Dorothy for not paying any attention to him.)*

19. What does Palmer feel is lurking in shadowy doorways and behind shaded windows? *(Family Fest and Pigeon Day are approaching.)*

20. What does Palmer think is good about Family Fest? What does he think is bad? *(He likes the talent contests, softball games, races, Tilt-A-Whirl, bumper cars, music, and food. The only bad thing is Pigeon Day.)*

21. What upset Palmer on his first Pigeon Day? *(He thought the wringer chasing the pigeon wanted it for a pet and was surprised when the pigeon was killed.)*

22. Why does Palmer conclude that all pigeons must be miserable? Why does he later decide his conclusion does not make sense? *(This is the only reason he can think of for why anyone would shoot a pigeon. He later decides that this does not make sense because his parents use other means to make him feel better, so there must be other ways to help miserable pigeons besides wringing their necks.)*

23. **Prediction:** Even though Palmer doesn't want to, will he become a wringer when he is ten years old?

Supplementary Activities

1. Critical Thinking: Palmer is going to receive The Treatment. Have the students discuss whether or not Palmer should allow Farquar to give him The Treatment. List the pros and cons on the board.

2. Art/Creative Writing: Palmer's hometown has a celebration each year. Have the students design a poster advertising a special event happening in their hometown.

Section Three, Chapters 9-12

Vocabulary

clueing (44)	smugly (44)	misery (46)	dashing (47)
bronco (48)	nuisance (48)	nuzzled (50)	tourist (51)
strutted (51)	smothered (52)	cooing (53)	wobbled (56)
bazookas (57)	intended (58)	fiery (59)	yanked (60)
skirting (61)	snagged (62)	taffy (62)	wrenching (63)
uproar (63)			

Discussion Questions

1. Why does Palmer ramble on about what happens to the birds on Pigeon Day as he is explaining it to Dorothy? *(It seems like the only way to get rid of the bad taste in his mouth is with more words.)*

2. Why does Dorothy run away from Palmer on her first Pigeon Day? *(She is upset by Palmer's description of what is going to happen to the pigeons.)*

3. Why do you think Palmer begins to cry as he yells to Dorothy that the wringers are only putting the birds out of misery? *(Answers will vary.)*

4. Why do you think Dorothy isn't afraid of Arthur Dodds? *(Answers will vary.)*

5. Why does Arthur Dodds call Palmer a "Sissymissy! Girlbaby!"? *(Palmer doesn't want to see the pigeon shoot.)*

6. How does Arthur Dodds make a nuisance of himself at the pigeon shoot when he is five years old? *(He keeps trying to get pigeons to wring, finally catching and killing one that falls into the picnic area.)*

7. Why do you think Arthur Dodds is so eager to wring the pigeons, while Palmer is not? *(Answers will vary.)*

8. What effect does the smell of gun smoke have on Palmer? *(He begins to smell it on his birthday and when he sits on his father's lap, even when his father hasn't fired his gun. The smell doesn't spoil his birthday or his father's lap, but changes them so they don't seem as good as they did before.)*

9. Why does Palmer stop playing with Dorothy? *(He thinks one reason the boys won't accept him is because he plays with Dorothy, a girl who is younger than he is.)*

10. How does Palmer's opinion of pigeons change after he sees them in the big city? *(He had heard that pigeons were nothing more than dirty, filthy rats with wings. After seeing them in the city, he thinks they look pretty with shiny coats and is fascinated by how they move.)*

11. Why is it now harder for Palmer to avoid Beans, Mutto, and Henry? *(Ever since The Treatment, they've shown him newfound respect and often come looking for him.)*

12. Why does Palmer forgive Dorothy for showing him no respect? *(She is a girl and doesn't understand anything beyond her hopscotch; also, he shares his memory of his second Pigeon Day with her.)*

13. Why does Palmer thank a pigeon when he is swinging? *(His father explained to him that Pigeon Day is a way of raising money for the park.)*

14. How does Palmer feel when his friends sneak into his house in the middle of the night? *(He feels honored.)*

15. How do you think Palmer's parents would react if they knew he snuck out of the house in the middle of the night with his friends? *(Answers will vary.)*

16. Why does Palmer go with Beans and Mutto when he knows he should not be out so late? *(He wants them to accept him and knows he has to do what they say to continue being part of the group.)*

17. How does Palmer react when Beans and Mutto begin hitting the crates of pigeons and open a crate? *(He tells them he has to go to the bathroom and runs home in horror.)*

18. Do you think Palmer's mother knows he isn't really sick? Why do you think she is so nice to him that day? *(Answers will vary.)*

Supplementary Activities

1. Compare and contrast: By the end of chapter 12, students have learned a great deal about Palmer and Beans. Have students create a Venn diagram (example below) to compare and contrast the two boys.

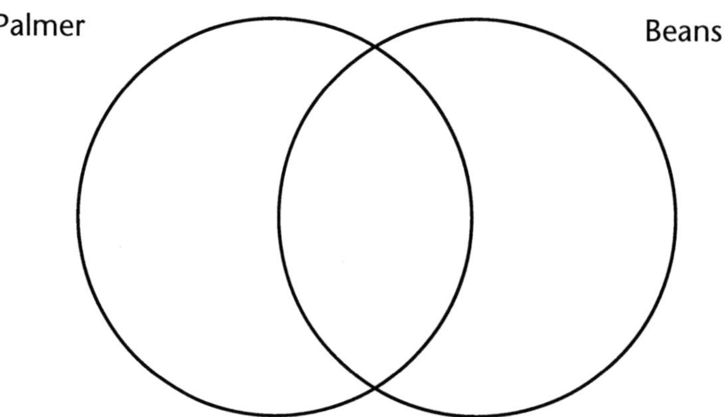

2. Math: Palmer sees crates containing 5,000 pigeons. To help the students visualize having 5,000 of something, figure out how many people attend your school. Students should divide the number of students enrolled by 30 to see how many classes are taught at a time. Ask the students to determine how many more classes are needed (or need to be eliminated) to reach the number 5,000.

Section Four, Chapters 13-16

Vocabulary

doozie (67)	blizzard (67)	classic (67)	Maserati (67)
adiós (68)	flakes (68)	grumped (69)	syrupy (69)
lobbed (71)	replying (72)	restraint (73)	concentrating (74)
plunged (74)	groggies (76)	persuader (77)	yelped (80)
scrap (80)	ambled (83)	swooped (83)	giggly (84)

Discussion Questions

1. How does Mr. LaRue suggest they "fool the weather"? *(He suggests Palmer put his sled away to fool the weather into snowing.)*

2. Why is Palmer disappointed about the blizzard? *(He thinks he won't be able to use his new sled.)*

3. Why does Palmer think that the bird tapping on his window is a dream? *(He often dreams of pigeons.)*

4. Why does Palmer think it is ironic that there is a bird tapping on his windowsill? *(Of all the towns a pigeon could come to, it comes to the one town that shoots five thousand pigeons each summer, and it comes to the window of the one boy who dreads being a wringer.)*

5. Why hasn't Palmer spoken to Dorothy since summer? *(He doesn't think he has room in his life for both Dorothy and his male friends.)*

6. How does Dorothy differ from Palmer's friends? *(Dorothy doesn't care about all of the mean rituals the boys have. She is not willing to do what other people say in order to be accepted into a group.)*

7. Do you think Palmer is disappointed when Dorothy does not invite him to her birthday party? Why? *(Answers will vary.)*

8. What does Palmer think might happen if he feeds the bird? *(He thinks the bird might keep coming back for more food the same way a stray cat would.)*

9. Why do you think Palmer decides to feed the bird? *(Answers will vary.)*

10. How does Palmer feel when he sees the bird did not stay even though Palmer fed him? (*First he is a little upset, then he feels good because his friends won't catch him with the bird, then he feels jealous at the thought of someone else feeding the bird, lastly he feels nervous because he realizes he is thinking of it as "his" bird.)*

11. What does the bird do in Palmer's room to make him laugh? *(It slips on a stack of comic books as it tries to land and flips over.)*

12. Why does Palmer do everything he usually does, but more quietly than usual? *(He thinks if he makes too much noise his mother will come to his room and find the bird.)*

13. Why does Palmer provide an explanation for why he wants his mother to knock before entering his room? *(He thinks she will be suspicious and snoop if he doesn't give her an explanation.)*

14. Why does Palmer go to sleep that night with a grin on his face? *(The pigeon is sleeping in the room with him.)*

Supplementary Activities

1. Art/Research: Have students illustrate two different types of pigeons to notice that there are different kinds. The pigeons should be drawn living in their habitat. Each picture should be labeled with the bird's name. Display the illustrations in the classroom.

2. Critical Thinking/Writing: Palmer gets a new sled but is disappointed because he is unable to use it for lack of snow. Have the students discuss times when they were disappointed. The students should then write a short paragraph about how they felt.

Section Five, Chapters 17-20

Vocabulary

earlobe (88)	nooks (90)	crannies (90)	skids (92)
routine (93)	stupendous (94)	maturity (95)	mushy (95)
scenarios (96)	cooties (96)	infested (97)	divert (97)
lean-to (99)	chime (99)	primitive (99)	recoiled (100)
flotsam (101)	Technicolor (102)	buckshot (104)	boundless (104)

Discussion Questions

1. Why does Palmer throw a blanket over the pigeon when his mother knocks on the door to wake him for school? *(He is afraid she is going to open the door and find the pigeon.)*

2. Why does Palmer think the bird is either dumb, clumsy, or a comedian? *(It lands on the comic books again and flips over backwards for the second time.)*

3. How does the bird react when Palmer lays cereal on the windowsill? *(The bird attacks the food, nipping at it.)*

4. Why does Palmer sneak a book about pigeons out of the library instead of checking the book out? *(He does not trust anyone in town, except Dorothy, when it comes to pigeons.)*

5. Why do pigeons eat gravel? *(They do not have teeth so they use the gravel to help break down food.)*

6. Why do pigeons primarily live in big cities? *(When pigeons came to this country, they headed for tall buildings because they look most like high cliffs to the birds.)*
7. Why does the length of the pigeon book surprise Palmer? *(He never thought there could be 89 pages worth of things to say about a pigeon.)*
8. Why does Palmer find it difficult to act normally now that he has Nipper? *(Palmer lives in a town that murders pigeons.)*
9. Why does Palmer tell his mother he is going to change his own bed sheets and clean his own room from now on? *(He doesn't want her to find any signs of Nipper.)*
10. What do you think Mrs. LaRue means when she asks Palmer, "What's next? Are you going to go out and get a job?" *(She is impressed because Palmer seems to be acting so responsibly.)*
11. How does Palmer use Dorothy as a diversion to keep his friends from finding Nipper? *(When the boys come close to Palmer's house, he suggests some way of picking on Dorothy to divert their attention.)*
12. What surprises Palmer about the appearance of Beans' house? *(The house is a lot nicer than he expects; it looks like a regular house.)*
13. Why do you think Beans is saving the muskrat carcass in his freezer? *(Answers will vary.)*
14. Why don't the boys pet Panther as he walks by them? *(Panther is the meanest cat in town.)*
15. Why does Beans put the muskrat in the microwave? *(He wants to thaw it out so it will be really smelly.)*
16. How does Palmer react to the sound of Mrs. Grusik's scream? *(It sends an icy buckshot through his body.)*
17. How do you think Palmer feels when Mutto looks up into the sky and claims to see a pigeon? *(Answers will vary.)*

Supplementary Activities

1. Science/Research: Have the students look up information about pigeons. They are to find answers to the following questions: What is the scientific name for pigeons? Where do they live and what do they eat? How many different kinds of pigeons are there? Do pigeons make good pets? How have the Armed Forces used pigeons in war? Do they still use them?
2. Critical Thinking: Beans and his friends call Dorothy "Fishface." Ask the students if they have ever been called names. Discuss how they would handle the situation. List possible solutions on the board.

Section Six, Chapters 21-24

Vocabulary

scanned (105)	deli (106)	prim (106)	reluctant (108)
carcass (108)	consequences (108)	scowl (109)	multicolored (110)
flinched (110)	spectators (111)	smoldered (111)	silhouette (113)
roosting (114)	raucous (119)	gobs (119)	dilemma (120)
clusters (121)	registered (121)	cackling (123)	phooey (125)
snickered (130)			

Discussion Questions

1. Why do the boys chase after the pigeon? *(Answers will vary.)*
2. Why do you think Palmer lies about the pigeon when Mutto says he saw the bird near Palmer's house? *(Answers will vary.)*
3. Why does Palmer break down and cry when he gets home from the deli? *(It was a tense, uncomfortable day. The muskrat carcass, the scream, and the pigeon sighting upset him.)*
4. Why does Palmer grab Nipper as soon as he opens the window instead of waiting for the bird to walk in? *(Answers will vary.)*
5. Why can't Palmer bring himself to wish that Nipper would fly to another boy in another town? *(Palmer is attached to Nipper.)*
6. Why does Nipper always circle Palmer's house before flying away? *(According to Palmer's book, Nipper does this to fix in his mind's compass where to return, but Palmer likes to believe Nipper does it because he is reluctant to leave.)*
7. Why do the boys stay away from Dorothy's house after the muskrat incident? *(Answers will vary.)*
8. Why does treestumping become popular among the other school kids? *(They notice what fun Palmer and his friends are having and decide to do it, too.)*
9. Why do you think Beans gets more and more irritated at Dorothy for ignoring him? *(Answers will vary.)*
10. What does Palmer realize after Dorothy asks him, "Why are you doing this to me?" *(He doesn't see her as a target anymore, but remembers that she is a person with feelings.)*
11. Why does Palmer think he has hurt Dorothy more than Beans? *(He and Dorothy had once been friends and had a special bond in regard to the pigeon shoot. He also laughs at her when Beans teases her. She is upset because Palmer goes along with Beans.)*
12. Why is Palmer upset when Nipper fails to come home one night? *(He fears something bad has happened to Nipper.)*

13. Why do you think Palmer chooses to share his secret about Nipper with Dorothy? *(Answers will vary.)*

14. How does Beans react when he finds that Farquar is not home to give him his Treatment? *(He runs all over town looking for Farquar.)*

15. How does Henry's opinion of The Treatment differ from Beans'? *(Henry hated The Treatment and had to be prodded to face Farquar. Beans goes looking for Farquar because he wants The Treatment.)*

16. Why is Beans so excited to be turning ten? *(He is finally old enough to be a wringer.)*

17. How does Palmer's mother feel about his renewed friendship with Dorothy? *(She is pleased Dorothy is back in his life.)*

18. Why does Dorothy continue to ignore Palmer at school? *(Palmer thinks she is ignoring him so he won't get in trouble with the gang.)*

19. Do you think Dorothy wishes she was part of the Beans Boys gang? Why? *(Answers will vary.)*

20. What does Palmer mean when he says that Dorothy makes him feel like "floating"? *(He knows that he can let go and she will hold him up. He feels safe with her.)*

21. Why does Palmer think it is impossible for him NOT to be a wringer? *(Answers will vary.)*

22. Why do you think Dorothy kisses Palmer? *(Answers will vary.)*

Supplementary Activity

Critical Thinking: Beans and his gang begin to treestump, tease, and call Dorothy names. Ask the students what they think about this situation. What would they do if they were Dorothy? What would they do if they were Palmer? Have the students write a short paragraph about the moral question of harassment.

Section Seven, Chapters 25-28

Vocabulary

bugle (132)	snipped (133)	crouched (134)	paced (136)
agitated (136)	tittered (137)	disguise (138)	anticipated (140)
mobbed (143)	detain (145)	immensely (146)	egged (146)
morsels (147)	spouted (147)	walloped (151)	rasped (151)
leering (152)	piped (153)	humanely (156)	jeers (157)

Discussion Questions

1. How does Palmer feel when Nipper lands on his head as he is walking with his friends? *(He feels like he has just fallen into a black hole.)*

2. Why does Palmer deny that Nipper is his pet? *(He is afraid of what the boys will think and how they will react if they know he has a pigeon as a pet.)*

3. Why do the boys believe that Nipper is Palmer's pet? *(Nipper landed on Palmer's head and they remember seeing a pigeon flying near Palmer's house.)*
4. Why does Palmer tell his friends he hates pigeons and is going to be the best wringer there ever was? *(Answers will vary.)*
5. How does Dorothy respond when Palmer tells her he "almost got killed out there" when the pigeon landed on his head? *(She tells Palmer, "They kill pigeons in this town not people.")*
6. Why doesn't Palmer want Dorothy to say the words, "kill pigeons" in front of Nipper? *(He thinks Nipper is listening to their conversation.)*
7. Why is Palmer both happy and unhappy when he finds Nipper at his window after his friends saw Nipper land on his head? *(He half wishes Nipper would leave so he will be rid of the problem, but he still loves Nipper and wants him as a pet.)*
8. Why is Palmer afraid to wear his regular clothes to school the next day? *(He thinks Nipper will recognize him and land on his head again.)*
9. Why does Palmer tell his teacher he has been bad? *(He wants her to keep him after school so he can avoid running into Nipper on his way home from school.)*
10. Why does Palmer keep erasing what he has written on the blackboard? *(He wants to stay after school as long as possible.)*
11. Do you think Palmer is glad his friends wait for him after school the day he is punished for spitting on the floor? Why? *(He probably isn't because he wanted to fool Nipper on his way home. If Nipper waited around too, then his friends may still see Nipper come over to Palmer. Answers will vary.)*
12. How does Palmer prove to his friends that he really spit on the floor? *(He dares them to go ask his teacher.)*
13. Why isn't Palmer relieved when he gets home and finds Nipper on the windowsill? *(He is too worn out by all the stress and weirdness of the day to be relieved.)*
14. How does getting in trouble at school seem to solve Palmer's two main problems? *(It boosts his popularity with the guys and it detains him after school so he is able to avoid Nipper on his way home.)*
15. Why does Palmer wish he were invisible? *(If he were invisible then Nipper would be as well, and his problem would go away.)*
16. Why does Palmer both wish that school is over and wish that it would not be over? *(He wants it to be over so he won't be faced with the problem of avoiding Nipper on the way home from school. He doesn't want school to be over because that means he is closer to his dreaded tenth birthday.)*
17. Why does Dorothy think Palmer is a hero in spite of all the naughty stuff he has been doing? *(She thinks he is a hero because he is getting in so much trouble to save Nipper.)*

18. How do you think Palmer feels about going to Wringer school? *(Answers will vary.)*
19. What is Palmer afraid the wringmaster will do when it is Palmer's turn to wring the stunt bird? *(He is afraid the wringmaster will realize that Palmer doesn't want to be a wringer and Palmer will never be able to show his face in town again.)*
20. Why do you think Palmer wrings the stunt bird instead of admitting he doesn't want to be a wringer? *(Answers will vary.)*
21. **Prediction:** Will Beans and the gang discover Nipper?

Supplementary Activities

1. Critical Thinking: Palmer is trying to keep Nipper from landing on his head again. Have the students explore ways that Palmer might keep Nipper from recognizing him while he is outside with his friends. List the suggestions on the board. Have the students vote on the five suggestions they think would be the most effective.
2. Art/History: Palmer wears an elephant mask to school. Take a class trip to the library to research the history of masks. How are they used in different cultures? How were they used in the past and how are they used today? Have the students illustrate a favorite or original mask and present it to the class and explain its historical significance.

Section Eight, Chapters 29-32

Vocabulary

impish (160)	sagged (160)	strategy (161)	traitor (161)
dopey (162)	waddling (163)	thrilled (164)	shimmering (166)
devastated (166)	smeared (168)	put out (169)	nacho (169)
foiled (170)	suspicious (170)	penlight (172)	cringed (173)
yelps (173)	tentatively (177)	airshaft (177)	

Discussion Questions

1. Why is Palmer worried about the sock? *(Palmer realizes that the sock represents a pigeon. In 28 days the Family Fest will host the pigeon shoot and Palmer will be expected to be a wringer.)*
2. Why does Dorothy think Palmer should tell everyone that he does not want to be a wringer? *(She thinks he would stop worrying if he told people.)*
3. Why does Palmer shut the window and pull down the shade after Dorothy yells out the window? *(He is afraid that Beans and the gang will hear her.)*
4. Why does Palmer consider himself Dorothy's best friend? *(Dorothy is the only person with whom he shares Nipper.)*
5. Why is it getting harder and harder for Palmer to stay on the good side of the gang? *(Palmer now fears the gang of boys. If they find out he has a pigeon, they will probably hurt him and maybe even kill Nipper.)*

6. How does Palmer think the guys will get him to lead them to his forbidden pet? *(They will torture him until he tells them about Nipper.)*

7. Why doesn't Dorothy come to Palmer's birthday party? *(Answers will vary.)*

8. Does Palmer's father think that Palmer should be a wringer? *(No, he thinks Palmer should decide for himself.)*

9. How does Palmer feel about The Treatment? *(He feels no pride, no honor, only that pain awaits him.)*

10. Why does Henry write "tonight" on Palmer's birthday cake? *(He wants to warn Palmer that the gang will visit him that night.)*

11. Why doesn't Palmer phone Henry about his message on the cake? *(Palmer thinks that it is too risky to phone Henry.)*

12. List the reasons why Palmer thinks that closing his window at night is not a good idea. *(The gang might keep banging on the window and wake his parents, the gang might get in through another window, or they might become more suspicious.)*

13. Why is Palmer worried that the gang is going to look in his closet? *(Palmer left the Honey Crunchers, Nipper's food, in the closet and is afraid that the gang will guess it is for his pet.)*

14. How does Palmer get upstairs before his father sees him? *(Palmer crouches behind the sofa and then dashes upstairs when his father goes into the kitchen.)*

15. How does Palmer explain to Beans why the word Nipper is written on the Nerf ball? *(Palmer explains that Nipper is his nickname.)*

16. How does Palmer explain why he has cereal and nachos in his room? *(Palmer says that he leaves the snacks in his room so he doesn't have to go all the way down to the kitchen.)*

17. What does Palmer see in Henry? *(Palmer sees that Henry is a captive, strong enough to warn him but too weak to do anything except follow Beans.)*

18. Why does this revelation scare Palmer? *(Palmer sees that he is similar to Henry and could become even worse.)*

19. Why do you think Farquar asks the gang, "You rushing me?" What impression do we have of Farquar? *(Answers will vary.)*

20. Why does Palmer refuse to take The Treatment? *(Answers will vary.)*

Supplementary Activities

1. Drama: Have the students reenact the scene in the novel where Palmer hides with Nipper as Beans and the gang come into his room.

2. Writing/Personal Opinion: Farquar is going to give Palmer The Treatment for his tenth birthday. Have the students write a composition stating whether Palmer was right in refusing to take The Treatment from Farquar. Students should support their positions with reasons.

Section Nine, Chapters 33-36

Vocabulary

whipped (180)	spectacularly (181)	blessedly (182)	precious (182)
wearily (184)	audible (185)	wicker (185)	transport (186)
spokes (186)	grazing (186)	sneered (187)	conscious (190)
deposit (191)	magically (192)	quivered (194)	bared (196)
privilege (197)	brazenly (197)	impression (198)	lurking (198)

Discussion Questions

1. Why does Palmer think a bug is crawling down the middle of his back? What is it? *(He feels something sliding down his back. It is really sweat.)*
2. Why is Palmer hiding near the dumpster? *(Beans and the gang are chasing him because he refused to take The Treatment.)*
3. Why does the worker from the GreatGrocer store give Palmer a can of Sprite? *(The worker tells Palmer that he looks like he needs it.)*
4. Why doesn't Palmer wait until dark to make a run for home? *(He is worried about Nipper coming home and being hurt or killed by the gang.)*
5. Why does Palmer decide that Nipper has to go? *(Palmer realizes that Nipper is not safe at his house anymore.)*
6. Why is Dorothy crying? *(She is crying because Palmer says they must take Nipper out of the neighborhood in order to save his life.)*
7. Why do Palmer and Dorothy tell their parents they are going on a picnic? *(They don't want them to know that they have a pigeon.)*
8. Why does Palmer want to take Nipper as far away as he can? *(He tells Dorothy that pigeons can find their way back from a long way.)*
9. Why do Palmer and Dorothy pull off the road where horses are grazing? *(They stop to eat.)*
10. Why does Palmer ride Dorothy's bike in circles, figure eights, zigzags, and crazy doodles? *(Palmer wants to confuse Nipper so he will not be able to find his way back to Palmer's house.)*
11. How do you think Nipper gets back to Palmer's house first? *(Answers will vary.)*
12. How does Palmer believe that the gang will get Nipper? *(He thinks they will sneak the cat in, spy on the house, use a slingshot, or maybe use poison.)*
13. Why does Dorothy begin to laugh and tell Palmer to walk back and forth? *(She wants Palmer to see what Nipper is doing. Nipper is pacing, turning, and stopping exactly like Palmer.)*
14. Why do you think Palmer's mother confesses that she knows about Nipper? *(Answers will vary.)*

15. How does Palmer explain how a new box of Honey Crunchers appeared in his closet whenever the old box was almost gone? *(He thinks that it is magic.)*

16. Why does Palmer think that his father will be mad if he finds out about Nipper? *(Palmer thinks his father hates pigeons because he won the trophy for shooting pigeons.)*

17. Why does Palmer's father come into his bedroom at night to look at Nipper? *(Answers will vary.)*

18. Why does Palmer stay in bed until noon after Dorothy and her family leave for their vacation? *(He is sad because he sent Nipper away with Dorothy when she went on vacation with her parents.)*

19. How does Dorothy carry Nipper over to her house? *(She refuses to use the shoebox and carries him across the street in her hands.)*

20. Why do Beans and the gang begin to tease and taunt Palmer? *(They believe that Palmer still has a pigeon.)*

21. Why does Palmer suggest that Henry come up to his bedroom? *(He wants to prove to the gang that the pigeon is gone.)*

22. Why does Palmer tell Henry to quit the gang? *(Palmer thinks that Henry is better than Beans because he has seen Henry be meek and kind. Henry does not have a mean nature. He pulls his little sister in the wagon and warns Palmer about Beans' night visit by writing "tonight" on the cake icing at Palmer's party.)*

Supplementary Activities

1. Art/Diorama: Have the students depict Palmer's bedroom including the pigeon and the yellow cat, or create any other scene or image based on the book. Encourage the students to be creative and to include as many details as they can in the diorama.

2. Social Studies/Map: Have the students draw a map of Palmer's neighborhood and surrounding area. The students should draw the pathway to where Palmer and Dorothy let Palmer go. The students should include a key and compass rose in their maps. Display the maps in the classroom.

Section Ten, Chapters 37-40

Vocabulary

cicada (199)	defenseless (200)	land mine (200)	platoon (200)
deployment (200)	crossfire (200)	fusillade (201)	regrouped (201)
semipro (201)	pureness (202)	macadam (202)	blotting (202)
tension (205)	reconstituted (205)	throttling (205)	intense (210)
pellets (211)	rotated (213)	sarcasm (223)	flexed (224)

Discussion Questions

1. Why does Palmer think the gang stopped coming to his house? *(Palmer thinks that the gang believes whatever Henry told them.)*

2. Why do you think Dorothy and Palmer avoid each other after Nipper is gone? *(Answers will vary.)*

3. Why does Palmer throw away the shoebox that served as both the soldiers' barracks and Nipper's roost? *(Answers will vary.)*

4. Why does Palmer bury his toy soldiers in the backyard after they have killed off the eraser in the make-believe battle? *(Answers will vary.)*

5. What makes you believe that Palmer is sad and depressed about Nipper leaving? *(Palmer no longer mounts the Beetle Bailey comic strips in his room, he never touches the Nerf ball, he doesn't play with his toy soldiers, and he sometimes keeps his bedroom door open and sometimes he keeps it closed.)*

6. Do you think Palmer is having a good time at the baseball game? Why or why not? *(Answers will vary. He does fun things but still appears to miss Nipper.)*

7. Why does Palmer think he can smell the future? *(He smells the odor of gun smoke from the cap pistols of four- and five-year-old children practicing to one day be wringers and shooters.)*

8. What does Palmer finally realize about releasing Nipper? Why? *(Palmer realizes that he let Nipper go for his own sake because now, Palmer no longer fears the yellow cat, he can sleep with the window open, and the tension no longer chokes him as it did for months.)*

9. Why do you think Palmer dreams about a pigeon that gets run over and then throttled by a wringer? *(Palmer is worried about Nipper.)*

10. How does Palmer feel as his father spends extra time with him and gives him extra attention? *(Palmer feels loved and cared for by his father.)*

11. Why does Palmer ride to the old train station to see the crates filled with pigeons? *(Answers will vary.)*

12. What is Palmer trying to feel as he stays near the crates with his eyes closed? *(Answers will vary.)*

13. What differences does Palmer observe about the shooters? *(Palmer finds that some shooters begin shooting at once, others are more patient, and a few shooters stand at attention before they begin to shoot.)*

14. Why doesn't the shooter like to kill a walker? *(A bird that is killed walking is worth no more than a wounded flyer; it is not worth very many points.)*

15. Why doesn't the wringer wring the necks of the pigeons in the field? *(It would take too much time. The wringer wrings the pigeon's neck at the sidelines and then tosses it into a large dark-green trash bag.)*

16. Why does Dorothy close her eyes and tell Palmer that she must leave the Family Fest shooting match? *(Dorothy does not like to see the birds being killed.)*

17. Why is Palmer upset when Dorothy tells him she let Nipper go at the railroad yards? *(Palmer knows that that is where the people go to catch the pigeons for the pigeon shoot.)*

18. How does Dorothy explain why she let Nipper go at the railroad yards? *(She tells Palmer that no one ever told her or her family about the place where the pigeons are trapped. The people in her family do not shoot pigeons.)*

19. How do you think Dorothy feels as she learns that she let Nipper go at the very railroad yards where they trap pigeons for the shoot? *(Dorothy feels sad and sorry about what she did.)*

20. Why is Palmer so worried about the pigeons in the crates? *(Palmer believes that one of the pigeons could be Nipper.)*

21. Why does Palmer look at the pigeon crates? *(He is trying to find Nipper among the thousands of boxes.)*

22. How do you think Palmer feels as he realizes that Nipper is circling the field in order to land on his head? *(Answers will vary.)*

23. Why do you think Beans grabs Nipper and runs with him to the shooting field? *(He wants to hurt Palmer by having his pet pigeon killed.)*

Supplementary Activities

1. Writing/Art: Palmer likes to collect Beetle Bailey comic strips. Have the students create a comic strip about the events that occurred in chapters 37-40. The students should give their comic strip a title.

2. Writing/Newspaper: The novel contains a newspaper article from the sharpshooter's point of view. Have the students write a newspaper article from Palmer's point of view.

Post-reading Discussion Questions

1. How might things have been different if Dorothy had not been Palmer's friend?
2. Think about the differences and similarities between Palmer's friendships with Dorothy and Beans. Use a Venn diagram to organize your thoughts. A sample is shown below.

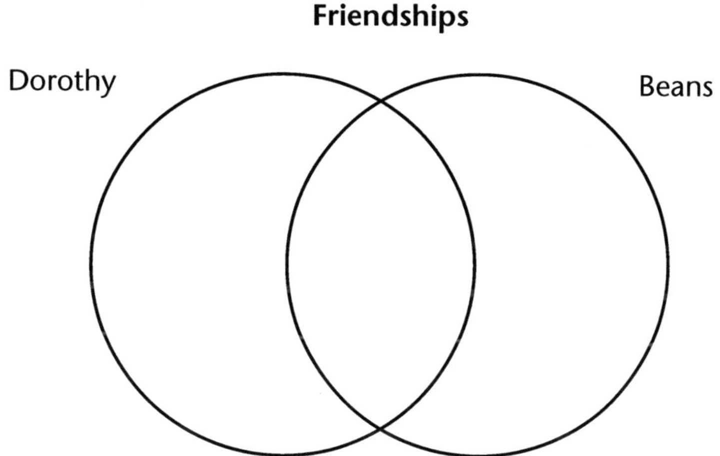

3. What important lessons did Palmer learn from having Nipper as a pet?
4. As you read this story, which character did you find most appealing? Why? Which character did you find most unappealing? Why?
5. Do you think *Wringer* is a good title for this book? Why or why not? Make up a new title for the story. Why would this be a good title for the book?
6. Have you read a story similar to this one? What is it? How is it similar? How is it different?
7. If you could change one part of this story, what would it be? Why?
8. Would you want to be a wringer? Why or why not?
9. How would the story be different if it had been told by Dorothy? by Beans? Palmer's mother?
10. Foreshadowing is the literary technique of giving clues about future events in a story. Where does the author use foreshadowing in *Wringer*? What clues are given? What future events are being suggested?
11. Would you recommend this book to a friend? Why or why not?

Post-reading Extension Activities

1. Write a short composition, poem, or song about how this story can help you in your own life.

2. Imagine that you are one of the main characters and write a diary account of the events of a particular day in the story.

3. Make a collage of the most important events in the novel.

4. If you were to meet Jerry Spinelli, the author of *Wringer,* what questions would you ask him?

5. The cover art on the 1998 paperback edition shows a mood-evoking photo of Palmer. Take photographs which express feelings the novel evoked for you.

6. Design a different book jacket or poster to advertise the book.

7. In small groups, create and perform a puppet show reenacting a scene from the book. (Puppets can be made with wooden dowels and styrofoam balls, socks, felt, or other materials. Be creative in your puppet design.)

8. If you could illustrate three scenes from the story, which scenes would you choose? Why? Illustrate one of those scenes and display your drawing in the classroom.

9. Choose one of your favorite parts of the story. Find music that expresses the feeling of the story at that point. Read aloud and record that section of the story on a tape along with the background music. Add the tape to the classroom listening library.

10. How do the main characters in *Wringer* change as the story progresses? Why do the characters change? What events contribute to these changes? Choose one character from the book and complete a character chart (see p. 31 in this guide) that shows how the character reacts to events in the story and how those events change the character.

11. Write an acrostic poem that describes one of the characters. Write the character's name vertically on a sheet of paper. After each letter in the character's name, write a descriptive word or phrase describing him or her. Use different parts of speech to describe your character.

Character Chart

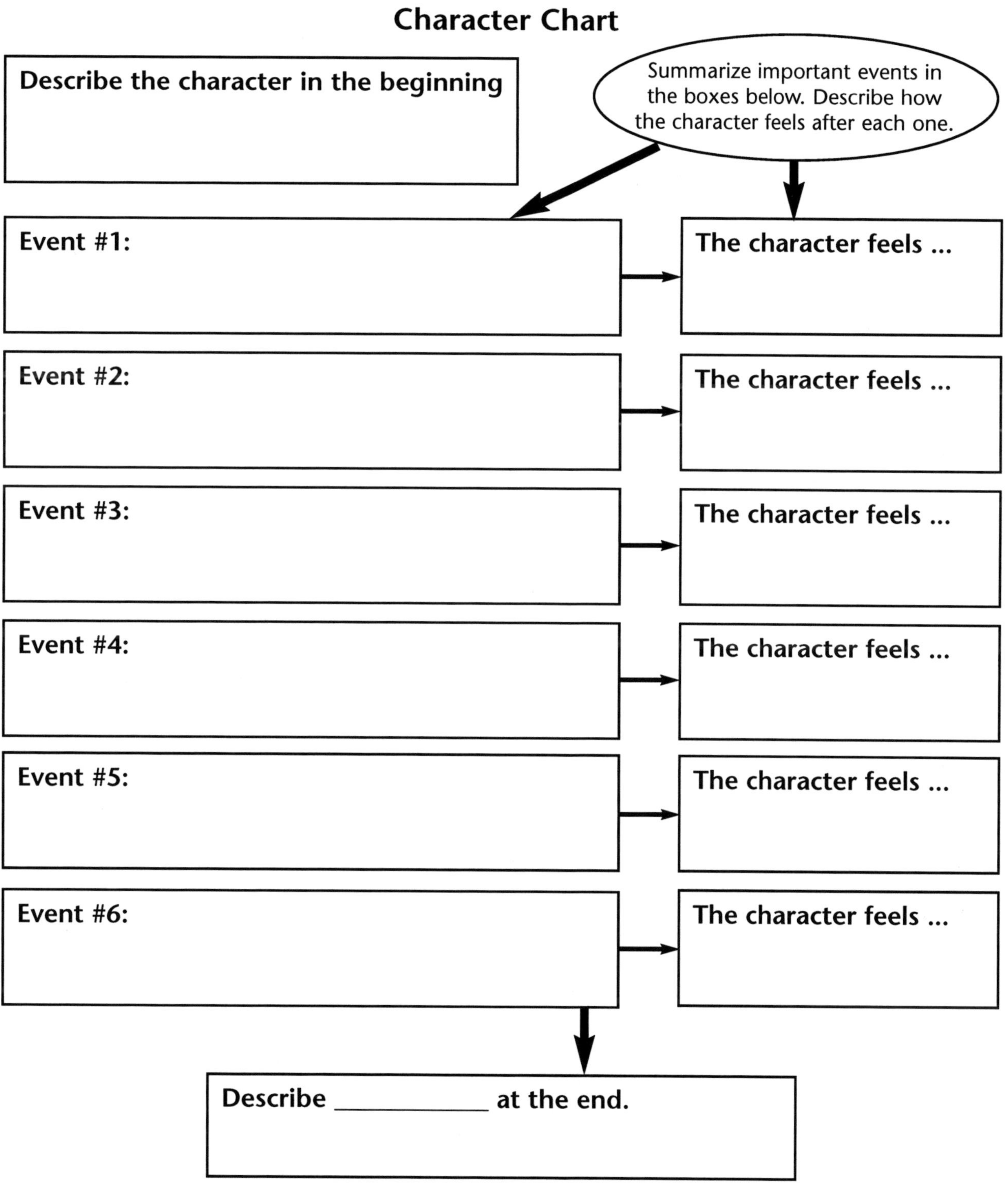

Assessment for *Wringer*

Assessment is an ongoing process. The following ten items can be completed during the novel study. Once finished, the student and teacher will check the work. Points may be added to indicate the level of understanding.

Name ______________________________ Date ______________

Student	Teacher	
_______	_______	1. Write a conversation that Palmer might have with his father about shooting pigeons.
_______	_______	2. Name one conflict that happened to the main character. List different ways that the character could have solved the conflict.
_______	_______	3. Would you like to have Palmer as a friend? Why or why not?
_______	_______	4. Find five adjectives and five adverbs in the story that helped create the mood of the story. Use at least three of the adjectives and adverbs in sentences.
_______	_______	5. Write a radio advertisement to encourage another student to read this book. Read your advertisement to the class.
_______	_______	6. Rank the main characters in order from best-liked to least-liked. Explain your ranking in a paragraph.
_______	_______	7. Make a character collage. Cut out words and pictures from magazines that describe one character in the novel. Put the character's name in the collage.
_______	_______	8. List at least three intense or sad scenes from the novel. Which characters were involved in each one? Why do you consider each scene intense or sad?
_______	_______	9. Write a letter to the author of *Wringer*, Jerry Spinelli, and tell him why you enjoyed the book.
_______	_______	10. Rewrite the ending of the story in the way you would have liked it to end.